THE (

GUIDE FOR

TEENS

DR. RITA BROOKS

COPYRIGHT

All rights reserved. This book or any portion thereof may not be reproduced, or used in any manner whatsoever without the express written permission of the publisher except for the use of brief quotation in a book review.

Table of Contents

COPYRIGHT 2

CHAPTER 1 11

Introduction 11

INSTRUCTION: THE HOW-TO-PLAY ESSENTIALS 13

What are the basics I need to know to just hit the ball solid? 17

There are so many different clubs. How do I need to know when and how to use them? 20

EQUIPMENT: EVERYTHING YOU SHOULD KNOW ABOUT WHAT TO PLAY................................... 23

How do I know if I'm ready for the golf course? 31

How do I get a tee time?............ 34

Where can I go to work on my game? 35

ETIQUETTE: THE BIGGEST DO'S AND DON'TS............................ 37

JUNIORS: THE BASICS FOR KIDS 40

CHAPTER 2 44

How to Support Your Teen Golfer 44

Help your athlete find the positives 45

Let them drive the goal setting ... 46

Consider when and how you talk to them about their rounds 47

It's Great to Start Golf Young But You Are Never Too Old 53

What is the Best Age to Start Golf Lessons? 60

And how many lessons are too many? 63

5 Tips on How to Teach Kids to Start Playing Golf 63

1. Make it fun 63

2. Involve them in lots of different activities 65

3. Choose the right equipment 69

4. Never worry about accuracy to start with 72

5. It does not have to be golf, golf, golf 74

Why Should Kids Start Playing Golf? 76

How to Encourage a New Golfer .. 88

Take a lesson 89

Be patient 90

Take the positives 91

Make sure to practice your short game....................................... 92

Don't put high expectations on yourself 93

Have fun! 93

At What Age Should Kids Start Golf Lessons? 94

3 to 5-year-olds 95

5 to 10-year-olds 96

10 to 14-year olds.................... 97

14 and older............................ 98

Benefits of Golf Lessons for Kids . 99

How to Find a Kid's Golf Instructor 101

Hiring a Kid's Golf Instructor 103

Supporting your Child's Love of Golf 105

Are You too Old to Pursue a Golf Career?................................. 106

The Greatest Golfer No One Knows 108

Modern Science 111

Modern Golf Equipment............ 114

11 creative ways to get your kid hooked on golf........................ 116

FORGET WHAT YOU'VE HEARD, START THEM NOW! 118

USE AGE-APPROPRIATE TEACHING METHODS 119

REMEMBER: YOU'RE IN IT FOR THE LONG TERM............................ 120

RECRUIT SOME FRIENDS 120

PUMP UP THE FUN FACTOR....... 121

KEEP IT SIMPLE AND RELATABLE 122

OFFER A MIX OF GROUP AND INDIVIDUAL LESSONS 123

TRY NOT TO OBSESS ON GOLF . 123

PLAY GAMES. LOTS OF GAMES! 124

GET THEM EQUIPMENT THAT FITS 125

DON'T WORRY ABOUT RESULTS 125

CHAPTER 1

Introduction

There has never been a better time to learn golf, and if you've come this far, it's probably because you've figured that out on your own. By its nature, golf is uniquely suited for a social-distancing world—it's a game played over a vast outdoor space, a worthwhile source of exercise, a diversion for the mind. To truly appreciate golf, however, you need to get past all the intimidating elements that might have kept you away until now. It's a hard game, for starters, and it brings with it an assortment of equipment and customs that might overwhelm anyone coming in cold.

To which we say, don't sweat it.

Every golfer has been a bad golfer at some point—many of us still are!—and you'd be surprised how much of everything you can pick up as you go. Our purpose here is to give you the basics—not only how to hit a golf ball, but what you need to hit the ball with, and anything else necessary to start your golf journey on the right foot (speaking of which, you don't need golf shoes right away). There's a reason Golf Digest has been around for 70 years, and it's because there's no shortage of topics to cover when it comes to the greatest game there is. But best to keep it simple with some basics here first. When you're ready for more, we're here.

INSTRUCTION: THE HOW-TO-PLAY ESSENTIALS

The Hall of Fame golfer-turned-commentator Johnny Miller once described teaching his kids how to play golf as starting out by letting them whack balls into a pond because it was fun to see the splash. Notably, there was no talk about how to hold a club, how to swing it, or anything else technical.

Does that mean you don't ever need lessons to get better? No, a good coach will certainly help you improve. Eventually. But Golf Digest Best Young Teacher Will Robins is firmly in the Miller camp, embracing the dynamics of the game first and fine-tuning later. That means going to a practice range, Par-3 course or even an open field with a sack of plastic whiffle balls and getting the feel for making the club move around you before diving into deep swing theory.

When you move from the phase where you're just trying to whack it to where you actually start thinking about mechanics, you stiffen up—and you probably have trouble even making contact.

Instead, stay connected to the feeling of swinging the club with some speed, not hitting "at" a ball. "You don't need a swing thought beyond: 'Get to a balanced finish and hold it for three seconds.

You can try Robins' video series, which helps get you off the couch and onto the course with fewer swing thoughts and more solid shots.

What are the basics I need to know to just hit the ball solid?

There are a blizzard of golf tips out there—trust us, we've seen them all!—which makes picking one that's perfect for you a tricky task.

A good place to start? You can think about a good swing motion as a composite of what lots of good players do. The closer you can get yourself to some of those benchmarks—without necessarily being obsessed with copying any particular player's swing—the more solid you'll hit the ball. Golf Digest 50

Best Teacher Nick Clearwater is the director of instruction for GolfTEC and has swing data on more than 50,000 players at all handicap levels.

Two prime examples keeping you away from hitting a solid shot that doesn't curve dramatically to the right? How you turn your shoulders back, and how you turn your hips through.

For a lot of new players, the tendency is to turn the shoulders back level, as if you were turning to look behind you to talk to someone. But tour players tilt their shoulders—so that the one closest to the target is lower—in addition to turning them.

You can also make solid contact much more likely with a quick tip for your hips. "Beginners tend to stall hip rotation—the amount the hips are turning toward the target—on the downswing and try to control the swing with their hands and arms. Tour players have their hips turned toward the target at impact almost twice as much.

There are so many different clubs. How do I need to know when and how to use them?

In broadest terms, your clubs themselves will help tell you when it's best to use them. Each club is designed for a particular job—namely, to send the ball a particular distance at a particular trajectory. The longest clubs in your bag—the driver, fairway woods and hybrids—have longer shafts and less loft on the face, so the ball goes farther and runs out more. With irons, the shafts get progressively shorter and the loft on the face progressively increases, which means the ball will travel shorter and come down more steeply as you work your way down from a 5-iron to a sand wedge.

The first secret to using each of those clubs well is to set up to give yourself the best chance of success, says Golf Digest 50 Best Teacher Cameron McCormick. "For example, with a short club like a wedge, you're trying to maximize clean contact and hit the ball on the descending part of your swing arc," he says. "That means the ball should be behind your sternum, or slightly behind center.

Contrast that to your driver, which should be played so that the ball is set up near your front foot—a difference of at least six inches. McCormick's Golf Digest Schools series works as a set of owner's manuals for the different clubs in your bag, and is a great way to get more of an introduction.

EQUIPMENT: EVERYTHING YOU SHOULD KNOW ABOUT WHAT TO PLAY

One of the intimidating things about getting started in golf is wondering whether you're using the right clubs. As with most things in this game, the key with equipment is to start slowly but strategically. First, even if most players get there eventually, there's no need to begin with 14 clubs in your bag. Basically you need less, not more.

You need a club you can hit off the tee on par 4s and par 5s, you need two or three clubs you can advance the ball down the fairway with at basically 100-, 150- and 200-yard increments (pitching wedge, 7-iron and a hybrid would be our choice), you need a sand wedge you can use around the green and out of the greenside bunkers and you need a putter. That's six clubs max.

Since limited sets are rare—you might get lucky with a used set, or on eBay—that probably means your buying strategy is to invest in a full set and pare down to the minimum number of clubs to get you around the golf course. There are box sets with a full complement of clubs for less than $200 in many places.

You'll need golf balls, but our advice at this point in your golf career is to spend less than $25 for as many balls as you can get. Once you stop losing two sleeves a round, then you can start to be a little more particular. Some other essentials we think are important:

Golf bag. Hard to find one that's decent quality for less than $100. If you're not sure about golf, maybe you should ask a friend who plays a lot if they've got an extra one in their garage. That will be sufficient for the time being, and it'll save you some cash.

Tees. These used to be handed out for free in piles but may be less plentiful today under the current touchless environment. Buy a pack of 100, and you won't be buying tees for years.

A divot tool to repair marks on the green will come in handy once your iron shots start to hit greens with more regularity, and you'll buy goodwill with playing partners.

Towel. Don't steal one from the linen closet. Steal one from your golfer friend who probably has 20 littering up his garage. It comes in handy to keep your clubs clean, and it helps when that chunky 9-iron's backwash splatters in your face. Trust us. It even happens to the best players in the game.

That's it, for starters. We think you can make this whole entrance to the game start for less than $500, and if you get creative, maybe even half that. Seems a bargain for the game of a lifetime.

OK, I've tried it and I'm hooked. What's my next move with my equipment?

This is a matter of defining how much of a commitment you've decided to make. And by commitment, we're talking about dollars and cents. While we highly endorse the used-club marketplace at the PGA Value Guide as a starting point, we know there's an even stronger level of appeal toward new clubs. (We especially like that idea because we highly value clubs that are custom fit specifically to your game.)

If you're not ready for the full couple of thousand dollars' investment, maybe focus on getting a new driver to start. That could mean a cursory clubfitting experience with an expert at your local golf shop. It could mean a virtual fitting like ones offered by some equipment companies (Ping and Callaway).

The beauty of a driver fitting is how relatively straightforward the experience is, but more often than not, you'll find you need a driver that is going to fight your slice. Some can be adjusted to achieve that effect with movable weights or hosels that can set the face in a closed position or an upright angle to help shots fade less. Other models are specifically geared to slice-correction, and again, let's emphasize a driver with draw-bias will not hurt the average beginning golfer's game. Not to start and not for a very long time after. You'll probably want a little more loft (try 10.5 degrees), but with the multiple levels of adjustability in today's drivers, you'll often be able to change that loft by as much two degrees (plus or minus) to dial in your performance as your game develops.

Why focus on the driver to start your new set? Simple. If you've got a driver you can trust, you've gone a long way to starting the hole with confidence, purpose and most importantly distance. That gives you a fighting chance to enjoy most of the day because there's nothing worse in golf than being out of the hole before you've actually started it.

How do I know if I'm ready for the golf course?

Can you get a 7-iron airborne off a tee with some consistency? Golf Digest Best Young Teacher Jason Birnbaum says that's the best way to gauge whether a beginner is ready for their first time on a course. And in fact, keep a bunch of tees handy even for the fairway, Birnbaum says. That's a great way to ensure beginners enjoy their first couple of rounds of golf. "You need to keep it fun," Birnbaum says. "Hitting off a tight lie in the fairway can be daunting to a beginner, so help instill confidence by encouraging them to tee up their iron shots. Using a 7-iron will give the player some good trajectory along with plenty of distance necessary to keep moving along at a good pace."

If possible, seek out a friend with golf experience for your first couple of rounds. They can really help with the minor aspects of etiquette (more on that below). The biggest thing, Birnbaum says, is trying your best to stay positive as struggles are part of the game for all levels.

Don't worry about what you shoot for your first 10-15 rounds," Birnbaum says. "Keep tabs of the number of solid hits versus poor hits. Once your solid hits outweigh your poor ones, you know you're on the path to improvement."

How do I get a tee time?

In the absence of access to a private course, you'll need to secure a tee time at a public course. Call your local course, and explain you're a beginner, and you're hoping to play when the course is less busy, thus making it a less pressure situation for you. Often, late afternoons are great options.

Where can I go to work on my game?

Practice ranges are great. We recommend finding a facility that lets you hit off grass once you've mastered hitting off a mat (hitting off grass is the most realistic practice, and mats will mess with your clubs). If you have a little room at home, setting up a net to hit into is a great alternative. Anywhere with enough room to allow you to make a full swing is a good practice spot. Plastic balls are great if you don't have a mat and are practicing in a field near you or your backyard. Those won't hurt anyone, and will allow you to take a full swing without losing a ball. Also, look into retail stores near you: Some offer practice time by the hour. That's a great alternative for winter practice.

What if I don't want to play a full 18 holes … are there alternatives?

Yes, always ask a course if you're interested in playing six, nine or 12 holes. Some courses allow you to pay per hole.

ETIQUETTE: THE BIGGEST DO'S AND DON'TS

I've always heard golf has a bunch of rules. What do I need to know to not make a fool of myself?

It's true, golf has plenty of rules, but you should take solace knowing even many experienced players don't know all of them. If you're venturing out onto the course for the first time, really the most important thing is to be respectful of the people you're playing with and the golf course itself.

For instance, it's worth noting most other players don't really care how good a golfer you are provided you're not dramatically impacting their experience. That means not slowing the round down even if you're struggling (better to give yourself a reasonable number of strokes for each hole and picking up for that hole after that). It means being mindful of not interfering with their swing by standing too close or making noise when they're over the ball. And it means leaving the course in decent shape for others: Replace your divots when you take one with a swing; try to even out ball marks on the green if you've dented them with a shot; and by smoothing out the sand in the bunker either with a rake or your foot if you've just hit out of one.

There are plenty of other nuances you can pick up as you play more (walking in between the line of another player's ball and the hole when you're on the green is one we'll give you now ... some people make a big deal about that), but if you go in with a good attitude and a willingness to admit what you don't know, most golfers will be happy to help you learn.

JUNIORS: THE BASICS FOR KIDS

There are a few ways to answer this, starting with the most straightforward: Simply take them with you the next time you go play. As golf courses have re-opened in recent weeks, there have been anecdotal stories from around the country of double the number of boys and girls playing compared to before the coronavirus. In part it's a reflection of many facilities relaxing restrictions on when junior play is allowed to cater to families looking for an activity everyone can take part in. Now more than ever, courses are looking to accommodate golfers of all ages.

More broadly, the best way to get your kids started is to make the experience as fun as possible. Have them play at first with only a handful of clubs. Don't have them hitting from the tee box; drop a ball (or tee one up) in the fairway around 100 yards from the hole and tell them to play there. Don't make them play every hole if they want a break. And don't worry about keeping score. The key is keeping it fun, and for them to associate golf with fun, so they want to return the next time.

As we wrote in this primer a few years ago (6 tips for taking your kids on the course), playing for the first time with kids means recognizing their attention spans are short. Embrace that so the experience doesn't drag out. Better for them to be upset they have to go rather than asking when are we leaving?

Our "How to play golf with your kids" survival guide also outlines a few handy secrets. Consider a different scoring system to increase the fun. Have them earn points for making good contact on each swing, or getting the ball out of a bunker. The more you "gamify" your golf experience, the more likely it will be the first of many for your kids.

CHAPTER 2

How to Support Your Teen Golfer

Use these tips (along with the other great things you're doing), and one day your child is likely to thank you for all that great support you're giving them.

Being the parent of a teen is a unique world (for you and them!). Your child wants independence, they're relying on you less, and they're getting ready to head into the world on their own in a handful of years. As exciting (and scary) as all that is, your teen still needs you in their life, especially as an athlete.

Help your athlete find the positives

Golf comes with tough moments, from sand traps to shanked balls, from high scores to bad tournaments, and let's not get started on tough coaches. With all of that, there is plenty of negativity that your teen can focus on, which means it's easy to lose sight of all the good things. Encourage them—daily, if possible—to find the positives. Cultivating positive thinking is a good habit to develop and they might need gentle reminders from you to see the growth, improvement, and positive moments that happen along the way.

Let them drive the goal setting

Since golf is a sport they can do for a long time, it's easy to start thinking about their future. Could golf help them get into college? Are they on a professional track? Maybe you see that they could improve their score when they seem to be coasting. Whatever it is, goals are personal, and if you start setting goals for your kids rather than with your kids, you'll likely see their motivation take a dip. Even if you don't entirely agree with their goals, try to let them take the driver's seat when it comes to setting the goals that are important to them.

Consider when and how you talk to them about their rounds

As parents, we like to talk about how things went. Sometimes in excruciating detail. Our kids just lived the experience, so they don't necessarily want to talk about the details, especially right after a round. Pick a time totally unrelated to golf to remind them that you care about what's going on and that you'd like to be able to talk to them about golf. Let them know that you also want to respect their feelings, so ask when would they like you to bring up golf and do they have any requests, like not in the car right before or after, but dinner would be a good time. Similar to goals, follow their lead, and you'll notice that your kids are probably willing to talk about it, especially when it's on their terms.

If they're not having fun, listen

Burnout is a real thing, but don't panic if your teen is talking about wanting to quit golf. It might just mean that they need a break, some down time, or simply more time to relax and have fun. They're at a point in life where their friends are very important and if they see golf as cutting into their time to have fun, well then, golf won't seem so fun. So, if your teen is talking about not enjoying golf, complaining about how much time it takes, or has lost motivation, consider making some short-term adjustments to allow them to get a little more breathing room in their schedule.

Teach your teens to manage their nerves

Teens get stressed and nervous; normalize these feelings and provide skills to help. Your athlete may have developed some stress management skills along the way, but they're still young, so stress and nerves can easily get the better of them, especially if they have a lot going on off the course (like around finals time, if they're struggling in personal relationships, or they're dealing with college prep). Talk to your athlete about using deep breathing to calm down and turning negative thoughts into positive ones in order to deal with nerves and stress. These skills can and should be used of the course as well. And parents, you can use these skills too—because being a parent is stressful!

What's the Best Age to Start Golf? Start Kids Young but Keep it Fun!

Now that my daughter is coming up to 2½ years old I have begun to wonder what is the best time to get her to start playing golf.

I hit my own first golf shots in my Grandma's back yard at the age of 4 and have not stopped since.

So what is the best age to start playing golf? Kids can be exposed to the game of golf as early as 2 years old. Research shows those starting early are more likely to play golf as adults. Formal instruction is generally better from school age (5-6) when longer attention spans enable kids to better learn the rules and risks associated with golf.

Children, of course, all progress and develop at different rates and what is right for one is not necessarily right for another.

But golf is a game for a lifetime and can be taken up at any stage of life.

And the key is how you teach someone to play golf, and by making learning the game fun you will give a beginner the best chance to get to a life long enjoyment of this great game.

It's Great to Start Golf Young But You Are Never Too Old

As with any other sport, it is best to start playing golf early, especially if you want to become very good.

Many people will have seen the video of the 2-year-old Tiger Woods on the Mike

Douglas Show displaying his ability to already hit a driver.

That is not to say it is impossible to start at a much later age and become a great player.

Greg Norman, winner of 2 Open Championships and ranked number one in the world for six years, took up the game at the comparatively late age of 15.

But by 17 he was a scratch golfer and turned professional at age 21.

But it must be remembered these exceptional players are the exceptions.

Golf is a lifetime sport and people have a lifetime to enjoy it.

There is also no requirement to become one of the best players in the world.

Golf is a unique game where players can be as old as 92 as well 2 and generations of families can play together all at the same time.

As long as you have a basic level of fitness and flexibility you can play golf.

That is not to dismiss the advantages of starting to play golf early however.

Kids who start young are much more likely to play golf as adults.

There is no problem at all exposing a child to golf as early as 2 and there is a school of thought that like skiing, where kids who are barely stand are already skiing, that a 1-year-old is old enough.

There are indeed manufacturers who make golf clubs for toddlers aged only 18 months.

There's a difference though between 'playing' golf and learning the game.

And while kids can obviously 'learn' the game – whether through watching it on TV or putting on the carpet at home – it is felt that kids need to be a bit older, 5-6 years old, before they are ready to start 'playing' golf.

Due to the equipment involved, there are opportunities for kids to hurt themselves and others.

Overexcited or frustrated youngsters getting hit or hitting someone with a golf club or golf ball are real possibilities in the early stages of learning the game.

So a certain level of maturity is required to know the etiquette and rules required to stay safe.

Golf also has a long list of often complex rules – Albert Einstein is reported to have given up golf after one try because he thought it was too complicated! – which children need to be a certain learning ability to pick up and understand.

So, the simple answer to the question of what is the right age to start playing golf depends on your child.

If you think they are mature to understand the rules at age 3 then great, get them playing.

If not you there is no harm in waiting for a couple of more years and just continue to expose them to aspects of the game in the meantime.

A lot of it will come down to how much interest an individual boy or girl has in the game.

If they are enjoying themselves chances are they will want to keep learning.

What is the Best Age to Start Golf Lessons?

What age to start formal structured lessons is another question when comes up when kids are learning to play golf.

Golf instruction, particularly in a group setting, is fantastic for youngsters.

Formal lessons are generally organised in a step-by-step format which greatly helps young players build their swing and associated routine.

Taking part in activities similar to their peers is great for friendships and the discipline required while young players follow the oral instructions given in a lesson will enhance their listening and learning skills.

The listening skills and ability to follow oral instructions are therefore key skills kids need to be able to participate in lessons so typically parents will enter their children into golf lessons when they are of school age, which is around 5 to 6 years old.

There is no hard and fast rule of course and if you are unsure if a child is ready for lessons you can simply sign them up for one or two and see how they get on.

If they are enjoying it, making progress and want to go back you can keep up the lessons.

If they find it difficult and stressful let them experience the game in other ways until they are ready to have another go at lessons.

And how many lessons are too many?

Again when the young player no longer wants to play is probably a good sign it is too much.

5 Tips on How to Teach Kids to Start Playing Golf

1. Make it fun

This is the first by far the most important tip when it comes to teaching kids to play golf.

If it is fun, the kids want to be there and parents are not constantly pushing and following their every move all will be fine.

Some golf events even introduce great rules to help avoid the over-competitive parent trap by requiring adults to be at least 70 yards from juniors in competitions.

Exposure is the key, and giving children the freedom to explore and enjoy the game, particularly, at very early ages, is paramount.

2. Involve them in lots of different activities

There is a myriad of ways now to introduce kids to golf in a variety of different settings and here are just a few ideas:

TV and Internet – put a sports channel on when there's a golfing tournament. You do not have to pick up any clubs to make them aware of the game and spark their interest in it.

Video games – these are another great way from the comfort of your own home to help kids learn the basic concepts and rules of the game, and also get to see what a swing looks like. Kids typically love video game given they are very visual and this can help them want to play the real thing sometime.

Miniature golf – putting is 40% of the game of golf and the miniature golf course is an ideal and fun setting to give them a starting point in golf and learning a putting stroke.

The back garden/backyard – at a moment's notice you can get kids playing and practising golf in a very familiar setting. Most back gardens or backyards can easily become a make-shift golf course with a bit of imagination and the help of a few hula-hoops, buckets, paddling pools and garden hoses. Just make sure you use plastic or foam balls to avoid injury or broken windows!

Driving range – before you need to head to the course the driving range is a perfect and safe venue to continue introducing kids to all the key basics of the game. Try and make days at the driving range short (no more than one hour) and action-packed.

On the course – children interested in the hame will eventually want to get onto a course but there are plenty of ways to gradually get them used to it and to keep their interest. To start with they can just accompany you to the course (riding around on a golf buggy is always great fun) and play a few putts or even chips when the opportunity arrives. Progress then to playing three holes or so, playing forward tees or letting them tee off very close to the green – no further than 100 yards out. Once they show an interest in keeping score establish an appropriate par for them remembering that pars and birdies are always better than bogeys!

Whatever you try just remember the main goal is always to fun and always playing games both in practice and on the course will hopefully mean they never get bored and catch the golfing bug.

3. Choose the right equipment

Choosing the right equipment will give kids a solid foundation, help them with their progress and prevent them from being needlessly put off.

Club weight and club height are the most important things to focus on to help kids learn the fundamentals and develop a good swing.

A lighter clubhead will allow more clubhead speed and distance and help with balance.

The height of the club meanwhile should roughly come up from the ground to reach an area between the waist and below the chest.

From the age of 2 kids grow an average of 2.5 inches per year so it is worth checking every now and then that their clubs are a proper fit for their size.

Non-slips shoes are also important to help make sure they avoid losing their footing during a swing.

It is almost impossible to develop a consistent sing rhythm if your feet are slipping all the time.

Another equipment tip is to look at some junior golf clothing.

This can help kids take more interest in the game and also start to learn more about its' etiquette rules.

Also when was the last time you did not like getting some new clothes?

4. Never worry about accuracy to start with

At a young age, kids are never going to hit the ball consistently straight.

So golf teachers advise never to focus on that aspect of the game.

Simply start with the basics and keep remembering always to keep it fun.

Teach them how to hold the golf club, where they should stand to hit the shot and how they should finish the swing.

Show them a golf swing and just get to try and copy and mimic it.

Encouraging words are also much more important than swing instruction.

As a rule of thumb aim for to use ten words of encouragement for every word of correction.

And keep things short and sharp and end your day with something special like a drink or snack.

This will let you all spend some more quality time together and introduce them to the great 19th hole where you review and talk endlessly about all the great shots you just played!

5. It does not have to be golf, golf, golf

The golf swing utilizes a diverse and wide-ranging set of muscle groups – at least 17 different ones.

Flexible and strong, upper and lower body, muscles are needed and must be merged with hand-eye co-ordination to keep a consistent swing.

So there are lots of other sports and activities you can do with your kids which will help prepare their bodies for golf.

Swimming, for example, is a great complementary activity to golf.

Not only does it increase flexibility but also contributes to core conditioning while strengthening the small muscles around the major joints used in golf – the shoulders, knees and wrists.

Athletics or track and field also helps train those upper and lower body muscles.

Football or soccer, basketball and tennis meanwhile lets them further develop the hand-eye co-ordination so heavily relied upon in golf.

Why Should Kids Start Playing Golf?

It is all very well talking about what age kids should start to golf but there is an inevitable question which comes before that of why should you bother teaching them.

Beyond golf being a great fun game to play there are a number of other benefits to playing to golf and here are just a few:

It is an outdoor activity which provides a safe and often beautiful environment for kids to play in

Golf enables children to develop their social skills as they constantly interact with different boys and girls of varying ages as well as instructors and other playing adults. Lifelong friendships are often fostered and developed on the golf course.

The game rewards perseverance, a positive attitude and teaches the benefits of never giving up. One of the game's greats famously coined the phrase – 'The more I practise the luckier I get' – and kids can quickly learn they are rarely one great shot away from rescuing a bad hole so it pays to try to never to give up and focus on the next shot.

Golf is renowned for being one of the only sports where it is expected that players will call a foul on themselves. Golfers are often on their own when rules are broken and are responsible for counting their own score. As a result, honesty is a key pillar of the game and expected of it all its participants.

Without getting too dramatic golf can also help teach some great life lessons. Like life, golf can be frustrating and again like life is not always fair. To get better the game demands you accept the ups and downs and as such, it can provide kids with multiple opportunities to learn how to control their emotions as they handle the inevitable successes and failures golf provides.

I will never forget the time my father walked in from the farthest point of the golf course after I had behaved appallingly.

After throwing numerous tantrums (and clubs!) he decided he had had enough and we did not then speak for the whole long walk back to the clubhouse or on the way home afterwards.

We also did not play together for a couple of weeks afterwards.

I quickly learned that if I wanted to enjoy golf with my Dad I needed to wise up and although my brothers frequently tell me my behaviour never improved I'm pretty sure it did.

My father never had to stop playing with me again from that point.

It is never too late to learn this great game.

It is truly a game for a lifetime where all generations of a family can play and enjoy it all together at the same time.

In our late 20's a friend of mine and I traded skills – he taught me how to ski while I taught him how to play golf.

Thankfully we did not put each other off and are still friends and we both now are still enjoying both the golf course and the slopes.

So long as you focus on making it fun there is never a 'right' age to start playing golf and it is never too late to pick it up.

There has always been talk at Aces about when is the right time for students to purchase a set of golf clubs of their own. Today I wanted to shed some light on the topic of buying your child's first set of clubs.

1. Experience and Interest: The first thing to consider is your child's experience and general interest in the game. I think we can all agree that there is no point of running out to your local pro shop and buying an entire set of clubs when you are not even sure that your child will enjoy golf. My recommendation is to start small. Enroll in a beginner golf course where clubs are provided and let your child learn the basics with minimal financial commitment. After your child has learned the basics and are interested in playing outside of class, consider a new or used set of clubs!

2. The Bare Necessities: The time has come, your child has or is currently learning the basics, is excited about golf, and you have chiseled out some time in their week for practice! Junior golf sets will come with between 4-14 clubs. Your beginner golfer will only need a basic 4 or 5 club set. All beginner golfers will need 4 clubs when developing their skills: 1 or 3 Wood, 7 or 8 Iron, Pitching or Sand Wedge, and a Putter! Lucky for parents today, the days of cutting down an old set of adult clubs are over. In fact,

Now there are so many junior golf club manufactures it is a bit confusing on what the difference maybe.

3. All clubs are created equally, but the manufactures are very different: In today's junior club marketplace there are many companies making junior equipment. From my experience, they are made of similar materials and casts. The larger differentiators in the manufacturers are the availability set depth(more club selection) as children advance and the ability to insure perfect fits as they continue to grow. We recommend our friends at U.S. Kids Golf.

When it comes to junior golf equipment U.S. Kids Golf is the hypothetical gold standard.

4. Getting the right Fit: Fitting junior golfer for the correct size club has always been a challenge. Historically many of the big club manufactures (Callaway, Taylor-Made, and Cleveland) have made there junior clubs to fit and age range. An "age" range? As you know from being parents you can line up five fourth graders and see that their heights can be very different, right? Please be careful if you are considering one of these sets, they can work, but must be fit by player height. Lastly, please note that players should not grow into their clubs. They should grown out of their clubs. A child swinging clubs that are too big for them (even if they choke down) can lead to some devastating losses in distance and technique. Choking down also introduces the subject of "counter weighting" and is another beast, for another post. In short keep it simple and use the U.S. Kids Golf Fitting System. All you need to do is grab a tape measure find your child's height in inches. Then pick the corresponding set!

How to Encourage a New Golfer

Playing a sport for the first time can be intimidating. Playing golf for the first time can be downright unfair sometimes. We were all beginners in the game of golf at some point and it's always nice when you have someone to encourage you, even through the bad shots.

As a beginner in the game of golf, you will hear hundreds of comments throughout a round of golf that you should ignore and some that may actually be good. Here are some things you should say to encourage a beginner:

Don't worry about it, get the next shot

This is the best thing you can ever say to someone who is new in the game of golf. Most people will strike the golf ball over 80 times per round and for beginners, even more. There is no point in dwelling on past shots when you have 98 more to hit in the next four hours.

Take a lesson

Going into the golf shop and asking for a lesson is tough for some people to do and it takes a lot of courage to admit that you are not very good at something. Most people have too much pride and they will never ask for a lesson. Telling beginners to take a lesson is the best thing you can ever do for them. Learning the foundations of a golf swing from a certified instructor can make the difference between shooting 80 and 110.

Be patient

This is the same phrase that we hear in all aspects of life, but it holds a special place in golf. Beginners in any sport want to get excited and see immediate results. In golf, you don't exactly see results until you have been playing for a while. Just playing a four-hour round of golf can take a lot of patience that most people don't have.

Take the positives

Golf is a humbling game and it will teach you a lot about yourself that you may not have known. If you don't take the positives from each shot or each round, this game will eat you alive. I know a few people who have given up on golf altogether because they weren't able to see the progress that they were making — letting the disappointments overwhelm them instead.

Make sure to practice your short game

Most amateur golfers don't even know where the chipping area is at their local course, and that's not a good thing. Golfers don't want to be seen chipping and hitting bunker shots. They would rather go bash 50 balls with their drivers on the range. Beginners need to work on their short game more than anyone else because it is the foundation of a golf swing. The movements that you make in the short game can be applied to your full swing.

Don't put high expectations on yourself

As a beginner, don't go out to a course and expect to shoot 72 or break 80. Go out to have fun and try to improve your game each time you go out. Having a number in your head of what you want to shoot can be devastating if you don't reach your goal.

Have fun!

The most important rule of any sport or hobby is to have fun! Who cares if you aren't hitting it the best on a certain day, at least you are outside and enjoying a day with your friends. You could be doing a lot worse for yourself.

At What Age Should Kids Start Golf Lessons?

At what age a child can start kids golf lessons will vary depending on the coaches in your area. Many coaches will take children as young as five, and other programs have higher age minimums. As soon as a child starts to show interest in golf is the best time to start teaching them how to play.

You can introduce a child as young as three to golf, and they can begin learning at home or by playing mini-golf. For older kids, there are even academies and boarding schools if the sport becomes a real passion.

3 to 5-year-olds

Children between the ages of three to five should be allowed to use golf freely as a form of play and fun. It's important that this age group not be given too much technical instruction. If you push, they may lose interest.

You should provide them with the right size club and show them how to hold it. Spend time with them hitting balls around the yard and riding around in golf carts.

5 to 10-year-olds

By the age of five, children may be able to join in on kids' golf lessons, individually or in a group. Group lessons are a good start and will teach them etiquette and sportsmanship.

Now is the time to make sure they don't start to develop bad habits that they'll have to work to undo later. Patience here will be necessary.

If they're interested in other sports too, it's essential not to limit them to just golf at this age. If their interest in golf continues to grow, they can specialize as they get a bit older.

10 to 14-year olds

For kids with keen interest, this age group can start to see benefits from individual junior golf lessons. This age group is when kids will also begin to transition from kids clubs to adult clubs.

Kids in this age group can also enjoy more options for golf programs, summer camps, and academies.

14 and older

Junior golfers aged fourteen and older will benefit the most from individual junior golf lessons, as they will generally have a greater attention span and stronger desire to learn.

There are many advanced options for golf lessons for juniors that they can now participate in at this age. There are numerous programs available for this age group if teenagers want to start learning to golf competitively.

Benefits of Golf Lessons for Kids

Playing golf is great fun, and children who play may only notice how much fun they're having. But golf also provides many other benefits and can instill important qualities in children that will serve them well in adulthood.

Learning golf takes excellent discipline. Children will swing and miss far more often than they hit it in the beginning. Golfing requires concentration and patience, and practicing these skills will prepare them for tough tasks throughout life.

Golfers are usually responsible for keeping track of their scores. Often, kids will have to keep track of their numbers, too, which means they must also learn to be honest.

Golfing is a fun way to be active and get healthy exercise. It's also one of the few sports that is gentle enough on the body that kids may be able to play for the rest of their lives. The fluid movements used are one of the reasons golf is popular among senior citizens.

How to Find a Kid's Golf Instructor

There are resources available online to help you find kid's golf instructors and programs near you. There are other resources online as well if you decide to go for a more advanced program or academy.

Ask for Recommendations

If you golf regularly, you probably know other parents who golf, and they may have coaches they use for their children. These parents can provide you with valuable insight into how the coach works, and what their results have been. They can also tell you what the kids think about the coach.

Social media is also an excellent resource for asking for recommendations. On these platforms, you can quickly receive information about multiple coaches, and people will often give additional insight into their personal experience with the coach they recommend. The information offered to you is all in one place, and you can easily compare and research from there.

Hiring a Kid's Golf Instructor

As with hiring any professional, there are things to consider before choosing the coach you'd like to hire. It's best to meet with the coach beforehand, and also consider visiting the facility to get a feel for the environment.

Consider the qualities you want to see in a junior golf coach. Bringing a list of questions can also be helpful.

Some things to consider in a coach:

How do they interact with children? See if you could have a chance to observe a lesson. Or ask if your child can meet with them first so you can see how they get along.

Do they primarily coach children? Or do they usually coach adults and take on the occasional junior? Do they explain technical terms in easy-to-understand words for younger kids?

What are their qualifications? What sort of training have they received in golf and coaching? How do they measure progress?

Supporting your Child's Love of Golf

Signing your child up for junior golf lessons is the first step in supporting your child's passion. Another way to show your support is also one of the rewarding -- enjoy golf together!

Spend time together at a course, watch golf together on TV, and take them shopping for new apparel. You'll make great memories together, and you'll show them that you support their hobbies and passions. Making memories is one of the most significant benefits of teaching your child to golf.

Are You too Old to Pursue a Golf Career?

Millions of people around the world dream of a golf career. What could be better than waking up every morning and spending your days on a beautiful golf course?

Not much, really; but obtaining that golf career isn't easy. It takes years of dedication to receive a PGA Tour card.

Nearly all professional golfers began playing the game as children and developed their skills during their youths.

But for a small minority of professional golfers, they didn't pick up the game until their teenage years or later.

Like most sports, a player's golf game isn't something that can be developed quickly, and it takes years to hone each shot.

With advancements in a variety of areas from nutrition and training to golf pro schools and professional golf college, there are ways players can enter the profession later in life.

The Greatest Golfer No One Knows

Larry Nelson wasn't an old man by any standards when he learned to play golf, but by the standards of learning the game for the first time, he wasn't young either.

During Nelson's tours of Vietnam, he began to learn how to golf at the ripe age of 21.

Nelson's introduction to golf wasn't the typical way most players find the game.

The Georgia-native was taught to play by a fellow soldier in the south Pacific.

The golf bug bite Nelson hard and the former high school star athlete studied the game every spare moment he had.

Upon returning home from war, Nelson dove headfirst into golf, and within a year was shooting under 70.

In 1971, the budding player turned his new hobby into a golf career at the age of 24.

Three years later, Nelson qualified for the PGA Tour.

Nelson's story would be great if it finished there, but it only gets better. The late bloomer won PGA Tour events and in 1981, as he had just entered his mid-30s, Nelson scored his first PGA major victory.

Two more would follow in 1983 and 1987 as Nelson continued a golf career that seemed unlikely when he turned pro in the early 1970s.

Nelson's story is one that shows it isn't too late to pick up the game, but what if you already play golf at a high level?

Modern Science

The evolution of sports and sports science has seen athletes prolong their careers for years longer than decades ago.

According to a 2013 study, the average age of PGA tour golfers is around 35-years old.

The good news from the research is players can still turn professional even in their early 30s.

It was also found that the best years for a golf professional is between 30 and 35, although plenty of tour players have shown they can still win tournaments in their 40s.

Mental and physical skills begin to decrease as humans get into their late 30s, so anyone planning for a professional golf career better have received their tour card by then.

Nutrition and fitness may not be the first words one associates with golf, but they play a major factor in a golfer's performance.

Like all professional athletes, golfers have a fitness routine and must stay physical fit to play at a top level.

John Daly may have won without having a true workout regimen and diet.

However, players like Daly winning on the tour is an exception rather than the rule in 2017.

Modern Golf Equipment

It isn't just fitness routines and nutrition that has helped golfers extend their careers.

Clubs and balls have been improved over the years as well.

Golf companies have continually redesigned their clubs to provide better distance and accuracy as players get older.

Balls are also designed with players and their abilities in mind.

Golf companies provide players with balls that suit them and these "provide a golfer with proper spin rate, ball speed, launch angle and maximum ball flight".

A lot of technology goes into the equipment golfers use, and the right tools could help a player begin their golf career much later in life or keep that career going.

Although there are ways for players to get into golf at a later age, it isn't the easiest task to accomplish.

11 creative ways to get your kid hooked on golf

It is a truth universally acknowledged that one of the benefits of having children is cementing the members of your foursome for life. Pretty sure that's what Jane Austen meant to say, right?

I jest. But in all seriousness, it certainly is every golf-loving parent's dream to one day join their mini-me on the golf course for hours of family fun.

There's just one problem: What if your little humans have zero interest in the game? It's a very real scenario these days, where school activities, other sports and screen time are all in constant competition for your child's attention.

So what's the solution? How do we guide our kids into golf's loving embrace?

As a parent of a 21-month-old, I have a vested interest in this topic. So I asked club professional Megan Padua, who heads up the junior golf program at the Maidstone Club in East Hampton, N.Y., and serves as a teaching professional at the Bonita Bay Club in Bonita Springs, Fla., during the winter season.

I have long admired Megan's devotion to teaching juniors. Here, in no particular order, are her recommendations for fostering a love of golf in your little one.

FORGET WHAT YOU'VE HEARD, START THEM NOW!

"I am all for getting kids to start at any age. As soon as they show interest. But as early as age two, you can have them swing a plastic club. It's never too young. I hear a lot of parents say they don't want to start their kids until they turn a certain age, but that time has come and gone. It's more about doing different things at different ages when it comes to instruction."

USE AGE-APPROPRIATE TEACHING METHODS

"When kids are first starting out, you want them to feel like they belong playing golf, that it's a sport they can do, and enjoy. Then, focus on skill development, but not necessarily technique. As they get a bit older, you can start doing some technique."

REMEMBER: YOU'RE IN IT FOR THE LONG TERM

"It doesn't matter how good your junior is, the most important thing is that they want to play for a long time. They may be the best 6-year-old, but if they don't want to play when they're 13, that's not a good thing. I like to get kids hooked on the game so they'll want to play forever."

RECRUIT SOME FRIENDS

"It's helpful, especially for younger girls, to have someone else to play with. That's important."

PUMP UP THE FUN FACTOR

"We do a lot of hitting water balloons. If a kid explodes a water balloon, it makes them laugh, because they're soaking wet at the end, but it also shows them that they can do that. At any skill level, you can break a water balloon. It doesn't matter if it goes up in the air, you just want to make a splash. So it also helps them with acceleration, and just making a golf swing, because you have to swing through it, as opposed to just to it. I also like to put baby powder on top of the golf balls, so it's like an exploding golf ball."

KEEP IT SIMPLE AND RELATABLE

"I like to use a lot of sayings with the kids, like, 'Give the grass a haircut.' Or, 'Hot-dog-in-a-bun grip.' I also have a little song that I use called the "Junior Golf Song." It includes all the essentials of the swing, and through the song, the kids already know how to swing when they sing it. I had a 6-year-old teach it to her 3-year-old sister, and next thing you know, the kid was able to do the whole golf swing, having never had a lesson before. It's a fun way for them to know the entire process of the golf swing.

OFFER A MIX OF GROUP AND INDIVIDUAL LESSONS

"Some kids love private sessions, and having someone you can relate to is really important. There's no exact time or age to transition your kids from group lessons to private sessions, but people should really expose their kids to a little of both."

TRY NOT TO OBSESS ON GOLF

"Letting kids do a bit of everything, playing other sports, developing values in all different areas and not focusing solely on golf helps kids become better athletes, which pays off in the long run."

When in doubt: replace a golf ball with a water balloon.

PLAY GAMES. LOTS OF GAMES!

"Games are really big for junior golf. The emphasis on games has grown more and more. There's a modern way of teaching juniors now, which focuses on athletic development, games, and keeping it fun. It's different than just having kids hit balls on the range. The U.S. Kids golf program, Operation 36 and the TPI junior program are great resources."

GET THEM EQUIPMENT THAT FITS

"It's really important that kids have the right clubs. Get them clubs that fit them, because learning with the wrong equipment can be such a turnoff. If the clubs are ill-fitting, it can make it so hard."

DON'T WORRY ABOUT RESULTS

"Put the emphasis on being there, the experience, and the fact that golf is fun. Adults worry way too much about how the kid is hitting the ball and whether their child has any potential. Golf is a 20-

year game, at least. Does it matter if your child has any potential? There are plenty of adults who aren't very good at golf. And there are so many benefits to playing golf! If you're wondering whether it's worth your time, of course it will be. It's the game of a Lifetime.

Printed in Great Britain
by Amazon